MIRACLES OF MEDICINE

VACCINES

BY VIC KOVACS

Gareth Stevens
PUBLISHING

Please visit our website, www.garethstevens.com.
For a free color catalog of all our high-quality books, call toll free 1-800-542-2595 or fax 1-877-542-2596.

Cataloging-in-Publication Data
Names: Kovacs, Vic.
Title: Vaccines / Vic Kovacs.
Description: New York : Gareth Stevens Publishing, 2017. | Series: Miracles of medicine | Includes index.
Identifiers: ISBN 9781482461022 (pbk.) | ISBN 9781482461725 (library bound) | ISBN 9781482461039 (6 pack)
Subjects: LCSH: Vaccines--Juvenile literature.
Classification: LCC RM281.K68 2017 | DDC 615'.372--dc23

Published in 2017 by
Gareth Stevens Publishing
111 East 14th Street, Suite 349
New York, NY 10003

Developed and produced for Rosen by BlueAppleWorks Inc.

Managing Editor for BlueAppleWorks: Melissa McClellan
Designer: Joshua Avramson
Photo Research: Jane Reid
Editor: Marcia Abramson

Photo Credits: Cover Alexander Raths/iStock; title page Evgeny Atamanenko/Shutterstock, p. 19 Evgeny Atamanenko/ Shutterstock; p. 5 James Northcote/Public Domain; p. 6 Public Domain; p.7 The Owl/Public Domain; p. 9 INSAGO/ Shutterstock; p. 10 Grook Da Oger/Creative Commons; p. 11 Asianet-Pakistan/Shutterstock.com; p. 13 Valeriya Anufriyeva/ Shutterstock.com; p. 14 anyaivanova/Shutterstock; p. 17 Alexander Raths/Shutterstock; p. 20 bikeriderlondon/ Shutterstock; p. 23 U.S. Navy photo by Mass Communication Specialist 2nd Class William Pittman/Public Domain; p. 25 USGov-HHS-CDC/Public Domain; p. 26 Thorkild Tylleskar/Creative Commons; p. 27 Thomas La Mela/Shutterstock.com; p. 28 CDC/Public Domain; p. 30 Russell Watkins/Department for International Development/Creative Commons; p. 31 Magnus Nortoft/Creative Commons; p. 33 National Institutes of Health/Public Domain; p. 34 FDA photo by Michael J. Ermarth/Public Domain; p. 36 Rocketclips, Inc./Shutterstock; p. 37 Tyler Olson/Shutterstock; p. 38 Nikolaj Kondratenko/ Shutterstock; p. 39 John Keith/ National Cancer Institute/National Institutes of Health/Public Domain; p. 41 Douglas Jordan, M.A./CDC/United States Department of Health and Human Services/Public Domain; p. 42 Sgt. Adam Erlewein/U.S. Army/Public Domain

Printed in the United States of America
CPSIA compliance information: Batch CW17GS: For further information contact Gareth Stevens, New York, New York at 1-800-542-2595.

CONTENTS

CHAPTER 1

THE HISTORY OF VACCINES

Vaccines are compounds, usually human-made, that are used to prevent the contraction of certain **diseases**. They are also one of the most important inventions in human history. They work by introducing a sample of a **virus** (usually dead or otherwise inactive) to your body, which then creates **antibodies** to destroy it. That way, if your body ever encounters the same disease again, it knows how to fight it off, and stops you from getting sick.

The first modern vaccine was created by a doctor from England named Edward Jenner. It was popular knowledge that milkmaids on farms tended to be immune to **smallpox**. Jenner thought this might be because they often contracted cowpox from cows while milking them. Cowpox is very similar to smallpox, but much less dangerous. Smallpox is often deadly, and is extremely contagious. Believing that a cowpox infection could protect someone from its more dangerous cousin, Jenner decided to test his theory in 1796.

THE FIRST VACCINE

THE FIRST SUCCESSFUL VACCINE WAS THE SMALLPOX VACCINE. IT WAS DEVELOPED BY DR. EDWARD JENNER IN 1796. JENNER NOTICED THAT MILKMAIDS WHO HAD PREVIOUSLY CAUGHT COWPOX BECAME IMMUNE TO SMALLPOX. JENNER USED THE COWPOX MATTER TO INOCULATE THE PATIENTS TO BUILD UP THEIR IMMUNITY. THE WORD "VACCINE" IS DERIVED FROM "VARIOLAE VACCINAE," WHICH MEANS "SMALLPOX OF THE COW."

4

FIGHTING MICROBES

Microbes are tiny organisms found everywhere on Earth including inside the human body. Some are essential for health but others, often called "germs," cause disease. When an unfamiliar microbe invades your body, the **immune system** tries to fight it. While this battle rages, you become ill. The more powerful the microbe, the more serious the illness may become. Vaccines have been developed to prevent many of these illnesses, but others still challenge scientists today.

Until Dr. Edward Jenner (1749-1823) discovered one of the basic principles of inoculation, smallpox killed millions of people worldwide each year. Although he never sought honors or financial gain for his work, he became known as "the father of immunology."

To test his cowpox theory, Jenner enlisted his gardener's eight-year-old son, James Phipps. Using pus taken from the cowpox lesions of an infected milkmaid, Jenner inoculated the boy. Phipps developed a fever and some discomfort, but did not become seriously ill. When he was later exposed to smallpox materials, he did not come down with the disease. This was a huge advance from the previous method of inoculation, which was to rub scratches with smallpox scabs, in the hope that this would produce a milder infection. Although it took some time, Jenner's cowpox-based vaccine eventually caught on and became the standard way to prevent a previously dangerous and deadly disease. Because of it, smallpox was declared eradicated in 1980. So far, it's the only human disease to have been completely wiped out.

Another early trailblazer was scientist Louis Pasteur. Pasteur was a major proponent of germ theory, and eventually convinced much of the world of their existence. Through this work he also created vaccines for rabies and anthrax. While conducting animal trials with his rabies vaccine, he faced a dilemma. A boy who had been attacked and badly hurt by a rabid dog was brought to him.

French scientist Louis Pasteur (1822-1895) made many discoveries about microbes and vaccines. He also invented the widely used process of pasteurization for removing bacteria from milk and other products.

Dr. Jonas Salk (1914-1995), an American physician, became a world hero for his work developing the first polio vaccine. He did not **patent** the vaccine because he wanted it to be available to everyone.

Since he wasn't a doctor, administering treatment, especially an experimental vaccine that had never been tested on humans, could have landed him in very hot water. Pasteur had him vaccinated anyway, and, luckily, it worked. The boy did not develop rabies, and Pasteur was considered a hero instead of being prosecuted.

Polio is a very contagious disease that's caused by a virus. In the late 19th and early 20th centuries, it was widely feared because it could cause permanent **paralysis** in some cases, and could even kill. Mostly infecting children, it is also known as infantile paralysis. It is also incurable. Epidemics were common in the first decades of the 20th century in America. Because of all these horrifying factors, the need for a vaccine to prevent the disease was obvious, but developing one proved difficult. Dr. Jonas Salk, building on previous experiments by other scientists, developed a new method. He killed several different strains of polio, which then became harmless. These were injected into the patient's bloodstream. The immune system then learned how to make antibodies that would destroy the viruses, without any harm to the subject. By 1955 the vaccine was approved for wide use, and cases of polio began to decline.

CHAPTER 2

TYPES OF VACCINES

There are several different types of vaccines. Though they all have different properties, they all function based on the same mechanism: introducing your body to viruses or **bacteria** and forcing your body to learn how to fight them off. Your body then develops an immunity to these illnesses without actually having to get sick. The degree to which the immunity-causing agent is weakened or killed depends on the type of vaccine. There are also vaccines that use agents other than viruses or bacteria. Different types of vaccines are developed based on the properties of the disease that is being prevented. Scientists determine which type of vaccine will be the most effective while also creating the fewest number of symptoms. Sometimes the type of vaccine used for a certain disease will change. This is often due to advances in medical science and the discovery of new techniques.

BIG EATERS

SEVERAL TYPES OF CELLS AND ORGANS MAKE UP THE IMMUNE SYSTEM. THEY WORK TOGETHER TO FIGHT HARMFUL MICROBES. MACROPHAGES, A TYPE OF WHITE BLOOD CELL, PLAY A BIG ROLE IN THIS PROCESS. THE NAME MEANS "BIG EATER" AND THAT'S WHAT THEY ARE. THEY HAVE A GIANT APPETITE FOR GOBBLING UP INVADING MICROBES. THEY ARE ALSO THE LARGEST OF ALL BLOOD CELLS, SO THE NAME WORKS ON TWO LEVELS!

The cells in your body are covered with molecules that show other cells they belong in your body. Invading microbes have different markers, called antigens. The presence of antigens alerts the immune system, which produces antibodies to fight the invader. Each microbe has its own special antigen. Vaccines work by getting the body to build up defenses to specific microbes.

Vaccinations use killed or weakened microbes to rev up the immune system. You don't get the disease, but your body learns to recognize and fight the real thing if you are exposed to it.

ATTENUATED VACCINES

Some vaccines use live versions of viruses or bacteria. However, they have been weakened enough that they are usually harmless to humans. They are very effective, because a live virus creates the most authentic immune response. This also gives them very long-lasting effects, with some giving lifetime immunity from only a shot or two.

Viruses or bacteria are attenuated, or weakened, through a few methods. One common way of doing this is to pass the virus through foreign bodies such as cell cultures or animal embryos. This process forces the virus to **mutate** into a form that can multiply in its new host, but makes it less able to replicate in humans. After doing this a number of times, the virus will be safe for humans, while still provoking an immune response.

Though they are very effective, these vaccines do have a few drawbacks. Because they use live **organisms**, there's a very small chance that the virus or bacteria could mutate and actually infect the host. However, this is incredibly unlikely. They also usually need to be kept refrigerated, so they can't be stored in places without those capabilities.

A/California/7/2009 (H1N1)v-like virus
Intramuscular use
Mix with adjuvant emulsion before use.
2.5 ml, storage (2°C-8°C), do not freeze,
After mixing with adjuvant emulsion: 10
Manufacturer: GlaxoSmithKline Biological
Rixensart - Belgium
suspension for injection
emic> <Pandemic> Influe

Some vaccines are used only during major epidemics. Pandemrix, a live attenuated vaccine for swine flu, is one of them.

An oral polio vaccine that used a living virus was developed in 1961 and used widely. The Salk-type vaccine is preferred today, however, because experts believe it is a bit safer.

COMBINED VACCINES

Some vaccines can be combined into a single shot. A good example is the MMR vaccine that is used to fight the measles-mumps-rubella combination of diseases. Combined vaccines are just as effective as single doses and they show no more side effects. Combining vaccines also means fewer doctor visits and less stress for patients.

It's fairly easy to create attenuated vaccines for viruses, but it's more difficult to do so with bacteria. Possible solutions include recombinant vector vaccines and DNA vaccines, which are both under study. A vector is a virus or bacteria used as a carrier. A recombinant vector vaccine uses a harmless vector to mimic a harmful microbe and provoke an immune response. DNA vaccines similarly use genetic material to stimulate the immune system.

VACCINES WITH INACTIVATED OR KILLED VIRUSES

Some vaccines are made with organisms that have been killed or made inactive. Bacteria and fungi, as living things, are killed, whereas viruses have their ability to reproduce inactivated. In these vaccines, the organism is still recognized by the immune system, which develops antibodies to combat it. Because they can no longer reproduce, they are considered somewhat safer than attenuated vaccines, since they can no longer mutate into a harmful form. However, the flip side of this is that the effects of these vaccines aren't as strong as live vaccines. They require multiple doses to create immunity, and they often also require occasional booster shots to continue working. This is because the antibodies created by this method can lessen over time. Because the virus or bacteria cannot reproduce, it's safe to give these vaccines to some people that wouldn't be able to receive live vaccines. One example is individuals whose immune systems have been **compromised**.

Heat or chemicals are usually the methods used to kill or inactivate organisms for vaccines. These methods destroy their ability to reproduce, but leave them intact enough to still provoke an immune response from the body. These vaccines are easier to store than live vaccines, since they don't need to be kept cold. Common examples of this type of vaccine include Salk's polio vaccine and hepatitis A vaccine.

A toxoid vaccine protects people worldwide against tetanus. This young woman was inoculated in the Democratic Republic of the Congo in 2008.

TOXOID VACCINES

Some bacteria create a toxin, or poison, that makes you sick. Scientists have figured out how to render many of these toxins harmless, usually in the same way they kill bacteria for vaccines. Once this is done, the resulting compound is called a toxoid. It works the same as other vaccines, creating an immune response to the toxin that the body remembers, but not actually causing the illness it normally would. Toxoid vaccines are very stable and cannot reproduce or cause the disease usually associated with them. Some toxoids require multiple doses to create immunity, but usually last for a long time. Common diseases that toxoids are used to prevent include tetanus and diphtheria.

SUBUNIT VACCINES

Both attenuated and inactivated vaccines contain whole organisms. Subunit vaccines are different: they contain only the parts that stimulate the immune system, called antigens. These proteins are usually found on the outer layer of a microbe. This makes them very safe, since they don't include any part that could actually cause the disease. However, this comes at a cost: they are not as strong as live vaccines, and your body might not remember how to fight the disease off in the future. This means they're often used for shorter-term protection, like in the annual flu shot.

CONJUGATE VACCINES

Conjugate vaccines, like subunit vaccines, only use part of the pathogen, not the whole cell. Some bacteria have antigens that are protected by a barrier. This stops the immune system from recognizing and reacting to them. In conjugate vaccines, the protected antigens are attached to carrier proteins that are recognized by the immune system. This then allows the body to react to these usually hidden dangers and create a response.

Scientists continue to develop new vaccines.

COMMON VACCINES CHART

The chart below shows vaccines commonly recommended in the United States, what they are for, and what type of vaccine they are.

NAME	PROTECTS AGAINST	TYPE
HepA	Hepatitis A - viral infection of liver	Killed/Inactivated
HepB	Hepatitis B - viral infection of liver	Subunit
Herpes Zoster	Shingles	Active
Hib	Haemophilus influenzae type b (Hib)	Conjugate
HPV	Human papilloma virus (HPV)	Subunit
Influenza	Seasonal flu	Split virus/Subunit
IPV	Polio	Killed/Inactivated
Meningococcal	Meningitis, blood infection	Active
MMR	Measles, mumps, and rubella	Live attenuated
PCV13	Pneumococcal disease — causes ear infection, pneumonia	Conjugate
RV	Rotavirus causes severe diarrhea	Attenuated
Td	Diphtheria and tetanus booster	Combined
Tdap	Tetanus, diphtheria, and pertussis	Combined
Varicella	Chicken pox	Live attenuated

CHAPTER 3
VACCINATION SCHEDULE

Most countries have suggested schedules for when people should be vaccinated. These schedules do two things: they recommend when to get certain vaccines to make them as effective as possible, and they take care of multiple shots in a single visit, cutting down on the number of doctor's visits needed. Some vaccines require multiple doses to create immunity, or eventually wear off altogether, which is another reason schedules are important. Doses are timed so as to continue creating full immunity, or to re-immunize the patient at the correct time to limit their vulnerability to disease.

Vaccination schedules can vary from country to country. This is because some diseases that are common in one part of the world might not be prevalent in another. Yellow fever, a viral infection, is a danger in parts of South America and Africa, so children in those areas are vaccinated against it. However, in the United States it's very rare, so it's not on the standard vaccine schedule. Cost and availability can also factor into this. Developing countries often have shorter vaccine schedules, whereas in developed countries, vaccines can last for years.

STARTING EARLY
HEPATITIS B IS OFTEN THE FIRST DISEASE TO BE VACCINATED AGAINST.
BABIES ARE OFTEN INOCULATED AT BIRTH!

If you're ever traveling internationally, it's a good idea to schedule a doctor's appointment six weeks beforehand. Your doctor will know of any necessary vaccinations you should get based on your destination, and can often provide them. Some countries even require proof of yellow fever vaccination before allowing you to enter!

International Certificate of Vaccination or Prophylaxis

International Health Regulations (2005)

Certificat international de vaccination ou de prophylaxie

Règlement sanitaire international (2005)

Issued to / Délivré à

..........or travel document number
.......cument de voyage

The International Certificate of Vaccination, nicknamed the Yellow Card, is used to establish proof of yellow fever inoculation. It also offers a convenient spot to keep all your vaccination records. The card can be obtained from a doctor or health department.

CHILDHOOD VACCINES

Most vaccines are administered to young children. This is because it's best to create immunities as soon as possible. The sooner someone is vaccinated, the sooner they are protected from a disease that could cause them great harm. So, as soon as a child's immune system is able to respond properly, vaccines are administered. The majority of inoculations start at two months. These include the RV, Tdap, Hib, PCV13, and IPV shots. They protect against rotavirus, diphtheria, tetanus, pertussis (whooping cough), haemophilus influenzae type b, pneumococcal disease, and polio. Booster shots are then given at four and six months, with additional boosters for some coming later. The MMR vaccine, which protects against mumps, measles, and rubella, and the varicella vaccine, for chicken pox, are given as early as twelve months. At four years old, the child begins receiving boosters for these two vaccines. The hepatitis A vaccine is also given beginning at twelve months, with a second dose administered six to eighteen months later.

This might seem like a lot of vaccines for a child to receive in a fairly short time period, but they have all been thoroughly tested and proven to be safe. Some people believe that such a rigorous schedule could overload an infant's immune system. As a result, they believe that certain inoculations should be delayed. However, there has been no evidence found that supports this theory. In fact, delaying vaccination lengthens the amount of time children could be exposed to dangerous diseases. This could have very harmful effects.

COST BENEFITS

When children are vaccinated, they get sick less, which saves their family the cost of medical care and time lost from work. A 2005 study found that each dollar spent on child vaccination in the United States saved $16 in combined costs to the family and society.

There are also vaccines that are given later in childhood, and throughout the teenage years. The HPV vaccine, recommended at eleven or twelve years old, protects against a virus that can cause several different types of cancer, including throat cancer and, in women, cervical cancer. Meningococcal vaccines are also recommended at this age. They prevent bacterial meningitis, which can be deadly.

19

ADULT VACCINES

Although most vaccines are given to children, there are still some that are recommended for adults. Some vaccinations do not provide lifelong immunity. As a result, periodic booster shots are needed throughout one's life. One example of a disease that requires multiple boosters is tetanus, which can cause lockjaw. It's recommended that adults get a tetanus booster once every ten years or so. Some diseases don't normally affect children, so vaccines aren't administered until they're at a higher risk. One fairly recent example of this is the herpes zoster vaccine, which can prevent shingles.

Adults also often receive vaccinations before traveling to other countries, depending on where they're going. These are for diseases that aren't a danger where they live, but might be more common in their destination. Travelers are often vaccinated for yellow fever, typhoid, and other diseases.

Going on safari or into any wild area can expose travelers to diseases spread by infected insects.

COMMON VACCINATION SCHEDULE CHART

BY AGE 2	
NAME	PROTECTS AGAINST
HepA	Hepatitis A - viral infection of liver
HepB	Hepatitis B - viral infection of liver
Hib	Haemophilus influenzae type b (Hib)
PCV13	Pneumococcal disease, causes ear infection, pneumonia
RV	Rotavirus - causes severe diarrhea
Tdap	Tetanus, diphtheria, and pertussis

BY AGE 7	
NAME	PROTECTS AGAINST
Tdap	Tetanus, diphtheria, and pertussis
IPV	Polio
MMR	Measles, mumps, and rubella
Varicella	Chickenpox

AGES 11-16	
NAME	PROTECTS AGAINST
HPV	Human papilloma virus (HPV)
Meningococcal	Meningitis, blood infection
Tdap	Tetanus, diphtheria, and pertussis

OVER 60	
NAME	PROTECTS AGAINST
Herpes Zoster	Shingles

SEASONAL AND REPEAT VACCINES	
NAME	PROTECTS AGAINST
Influenza	Seasonal flu
Td	Diphtheria and tetanus 10-year booster

2

SIDE EFFECTS AND EFFECTIVENESS

Vaccines are extremely safe. However, they can on occasion have negative side effects. These are called adverse effects. Most adverse effects are not serious. They can include redness, soreness, and/or swelling at the injection point. Mild, flu-like symptoms can also occur. These might include fever, nausea, tiredness, headache, and even vomiting. This is because vaccines train your body to fight off illnesses. The immune response to vaccines sometimes provokes flu-like symptoms, but they are much more mild than what the disease would actually do. Most of these symptoms go away in a day or so.

Occasionally, serious adverse effects can occur. Though rare, they can be dangerous, and a doctor should be consulted if they develop. Serious adverse effects can include severe allergic reactions, including difficulty breathing, facial swelling, and lowered blood pressure. Other serious adverse effects include seizures, joint pain and stiffness, and pneumonia.

Vaccines are one of the most effective forms of modern medicine. No vaccine can claim 100% effectiveness, but most are very close. The majority of childhood vaccines impart immunity between 90% and 100% of the time. Thanks to vaccines, cases of diseases like mumps, measles, and polio have been almost completely eliminated.

Influenza used to spread widely on US military bases, but now all personnel and their families receive annual immunizations.

FIGHTING THE FLU, YEAR BY YEAR

One vaccine that doctors recommend people get every year is the flu shot. Babies can start getting it at six months, and it's recommended that you get one annually. Scientists actually develop a new flu shot every year, for a few reasons. The influenza virus is constantly mutating. This means that the virus that's getting people sick this year might be very different from the one you were vaccinated for last year. Your antibodies have also probably decreased since your previous shot, so a reminder for your body helps. Because it's impossible to predict which flu virus will be most common in a given year, scientists have to make an educated guess. The most common flu vaccines contain three or four different flu viruses that scientists believe will be the most common that season. This means that some years the vaccine is more effective than others, but it's always a good idea to get the shot. After all, some protection is better than none.

There will probably never be a vaccine that is completely without risk or that creates total immunity in 100% of subjects. For the vast majority of people, though, vaccines are a safe, effective way to prevent painful, often deadly diseases. Scientists are also working constantly to develop new, safer, and more effective vaccines.

CHAPTER 4
PUBLIC HEALTH

Vaccines are one of the greatest tools available to ensure and protect the general health of the public. The greater number of people vaccinated, the fewer there are getting sick. This also leads to fewer diseases spreading. Vaccines have greatly cut down on the number of epidemics, especially in developed countries. Diseases that once ravaged huge parts of the population are now fairly rare.

Most countries have groups that oversee the scheduling and implementation of vaccine programs. In the United States, this is the Centers for Disease Control, or the CDC. Diseases don't care about national borders, though. This has led to a number of organizations that coordinate programs internationally. These efforts are important, since they focus on stopping diseases globally, instead of in just one geographic area. The World Health Organization, or WHO, is a leader in this field.

The intent of all of these organizations, national and international alike, is to stop disease. There are two levels of this stoppage: elimination and eradication. For a disease to be considered eliminated, it has to no longer be spreading in a certain area, like a country or a continent. In both the United States and Europe, polio has been eliminated. It is still present elsewhere, but its spread has been contained in those locales.

Though the vaccine was developed in 1796, it took nearly 200 years to win the fight against smallpox. As late as the 1960s, Africa and Asia suffered many cases each year. Health officials and governments worldwide teamed up for a massive effort including vaccination campaigns and other prevention measures. And it worked. In 1980, they were able to declare smallpox eradicated.

In 1980, three former directors of the Global Smallpox Eradication Program shared the good news that the work started by Edward Jenner was completed with the official end of smallpox.

Eradication is a step up from elimination. It is the total destruction of a disease's ability to spread globally. So far, only smallpox has been totally eradicated. Because smallpox no longer exists in nature, there is no longer a need to vaccinate against it.

WHO'S EXPANDED PROGRAM ON IMMUNIZATION (EPI)

The World Health Organization came together in 1948 as a specialized agency of the United Nations. Broadly, it aims to improve the health and well-being of people everywhere, through a variety of means. It provides information and tracks health statistics the world over, helps to implement systems that lead to greater overall health, and much more. In its efforts throughout its existence to combat communicable diseases, it has been a major proponent of vaccines.

The World Health Organization has 194 member nations whose health ministers meet each year in Geneva, Switzerland. WHO also has offices providing help in most of those countries.

HERD IMMUNITY

Some people cannot receive vaccines. They might be too young, they might have allergies, or they might have an immune disorder that prevents it. For these people, herd immunity is a very important form of protection from disease. Herd immunity, also known as community immunity, happens when the majority of a population are vaccinated against, or otherwise immune to a disease. That way, even if an infected person comes into contact with the population, most of its members cannot spread the disease. This helps to keep people who can't receive vaccines safe and healthy. The fewer people that are vaccinated, the lower herd immunity is, and the more people are likely to get sick.

The WHO started the Expanded Program on Immunization (EPI) in 1974. Its goal was to increase the number of children being vaccinated around the world. In 1977, it specifically targeted six diseases: diphtheria, measles, pertussis, tetanus, polio, and tuberculosis. Before the EPI, less than 5% of kids received vaccinations. Now, that number is almost 80%! The scope of the program has also been widened to target yellow fever, Hib, and hepatitis B.

YELLOW FEVER

Yellow fever started in Africa and traveled to the Americas with the slave trade. Mosquitoes spread the disease, which is called yellow fever because it can cause liver jaundice that turns the skin yellow. Most people experience fevers and headaches, but about 30 percent develop severe symptoms including jaundice, vomiting, and bleeding from the skin. About half of these people die.

A Cuban doctor discovered in 1881 that exterminating mosquitoes helped control the disease. In 1937, a safe and affordable vaccine was developed. Even so, major outbreaks remain a threat in the areas highlighted on the maps below, especially in Africa. In 2006, world health officials launched the Yellow Fever Initiative there. More than 105 million people have been vaccinated so far but sporadic outbreaks continue, including a serious one in Angola in 2016.

One inoculation provides immunity for a lifetime but there is still no cure for yellow fever itself.

■ Regions in Africa still affected by yellow fever

■ Regions in South America still affected by yellow fever

The EPI continues to pursue its goals, which include globally eradicating polio, and ensuring total immunization for children under a year old all over the planet. It works towards these goals by establishing guidelines that are followed by member countries, and by helping to improve access to vaccines, no matter where a child might be.

GLOBAL ALLIANCE FOR VACCINES AND IMMUNIZATION (GAVI)

The Global Alliance for Vaccines and Immunization (known today as the GAVI Alliance) was created in 2000. Its goal is to increase the availability of vaccines in the world's poorest countries. It started at a time when immunization rates in some countries had stopped growing, or, in some cases, started to fall. It brings groups such as WHO and the United Nations Children's Fund (UNICEF) together with national governments, philanthropic organizations, and members of the private sector. This collaboration has increased both the number of children being vaccinated and the number of vaccines available to them. The alliance has been able to greatly decrease the amount of time it takes for vaccines to reach developing countries after being developed. These efforts have prevented over 5 million deaths, and have led to the vaccination of hundreds of millions of children.

THE ANTI-VACCINES MOVEMENT (ANTI-VAXXERS)

Vaccines have been controversial for as long as they've existed. Beginning with Edward Jenner's smallpox vaccine, people have been opposed to them for a variety of reasons. Religious opposition was common, as were sanitary concerns. When mandatory vaccination laws started to be passed, many people resented not having a choice in the matter.

As new vaccines became common in the 20th century, new concerns were raised. SV-40, a disease that can affect both monkeys and humans, was found in both the Salk and Sabin polio vaccines from 1955 until 1963. The virus can lead to certain cancers in humans, but the vaccinated and unvaccinated populations of the time show the same cancer rates.

One of the biggest fears connected with vaccines is that they somehow cause autism. This belief can be traced back to a 1998 study by British doctor Andrew Wakefield and a dozen colleagues in the Lancet, a medical journal. The paper claimed that twelve children developed autism symptoms, as well as intestinal problems. However, since its publication, ten of its coauthors have withdrawn their support of its conclusions, and the Lancet has retracted the study.

Feelings run high about vaccination, though most people believe the benefits far outweigh any risks. This pro-vaccine march was held in London.

Wakefield was found to have a conflict of interest after it was revealed he had filed a patent for his own version of the measles vaccine, and had accepted money from lawyers who were suing the vaccine manufacturers on behalf of some of the children in his study. He was also found to have tampered with his data.

Despite all this, the belief in a connection between vaccines and autism still exists. Some people believe a preservative in some vaccines, thimerosal, is the cause. They point to the fact that it contains mercury, which in high doses can be deadly. Despite the fact that the amounts in vaccines have been shown to be safe, the ingredient was removed in vaccines for infants, starting in 1999. Since then, its removal has not been shown to lead to fewer cases of autism. Over and over again, studies have been unable to show a link between vaccines and autism.

Ironically, part of the reason many people no longer believe vaccines are necessary is because they have been so effective. Generations that haven't grown up with the devastating effects of diseases like polio and measles don't understand how serious their effects can be. Alternative medicine has also gained in popularity, and often espouses alternate treatments that have no basis in science.

There will probably never be a vaccine that is 100% risk-free and effective. However, the vast majority of medical professionals and scientists agree that vaccines are an important part of developing long-term health in the overwhelming majority of the population.

CHAPTER 5

CREATING VACCINES

Creating a new vaccine is a lengthy process with several steps. It often takes over ten years for a vaccine to go from development to actual production. Though this might seem like a long time, it's absolutely vital to ensure that the vaccine is as effective and safe as possible. After all, the human immune system is an incredibly complex machine, and figuring out how to create the best response in it takes both time and experimentation. Vaccine creation is highly regulated to ensure proper steps are taken throughout the process.

In the United States, the Food and Drug Administration (FDA) oversees the development, production, and safety of vaccines. This federal agency is part of the Department of Health and Human Services.

The FDA's mission to keep vaccines safe does not end once consumers begin receiving their inoculations. As with all medical products, the manufacturer must adhere to strict standards of safety and cleanliness.

SAFETY FIRST

TO KEEP PEOPLE SAFE, IT TAKES TEN TO FIFTEEN YEARS OF TESTING BEFORE A VACCINE REACHES THE PUBLIC. LENGTHY CLINICAL TRIALS ARE CONDUCTED ON HEALTHY HUMAN VOLUNTEERS, FIRST IN SMALL GROUPS AND THEN BY THE THOUSANDS. ONCE APPROVED, VACCINES STILL ARE MONITORED CLOSELY BY FDA AND WORLD HEALTH OFFICIALS.

Vaccine makers need a license for each new vaccine before it can be used in the United States. To get a license, they submit a Biologics License Application (BLA) affirming that the vaccine is safe and effective. Then a panel of FDA experts and an advisory committee of doctors, scientists, and consumer representatives must approve the license.

During the 2014 Ebola virus outbreak, President Barack Obama got a briefing from Dr. Nancy Sullivan about work on a vaccine at the Vaccine Research Center in Maryland.

More than 200 branch offices and labs throughout the United States help the FDA monitor product safety.

The vaccine maker, the FDA, and the Centers for Disease Control and Prevention (CDC) also continue to work closely to monitor any reports of side effects, from simple symptoms to life-threatening conditions. Sometimes a vaccine or drug must be pulled from the market because of complications.

DEVELOPMENT

Before they can start creating a vaccine, scientists first have to understand the organism that causes the disease. This research allows them to determine what kind of vaccine should be developed. Is the disease caused by a virus or bacteria? If it's bacteria, would a toxoid vaccine be the best choice? Once they're familiar with the disease, researchers then figure out which antigens will provoke an immune response. These could be natural or human-made.

Once this research has been done, the preclinical stage begins. In this stage, the new vaccine is tested using tissue-culture or cell-culture samples in test tubes. Animal testing also takes place in this time frame. Monkeys and mice are commonly used in these trials. Human tests are still a number of steps away. During animal testing, a procedure called a challenge test is often done. After giving a vaccine to an animal, scientists will then deliberately try to infect it with the disease. If it doesn't become ill, it shows that the vaccine has helped to create an immunity.

TRIALS

At this point, one of two things could happen. If the vaccine doesn't seem to be creating the desired response, research stops, and it's back to the drawing board. If it does seem to be creating immunity, an application is made to the FDA for permission to begin clinical trials. In the United States, this is called an Investigational New Drug (IND) application. Part of the application is presenting both the research that has been done, and the future research scientists wish to pursue. If the researchers receive the go-ahead from a committee, clinical trials begin.

Clinical trials involve human testing, and take place in three phases. In Phase I, between 20 to 80 adults are tested. Adults are used even if the vaccine is intended for children.

If these initial trials are successful, younger subjects are gradually used until they reach the target age. Often in these trials some subjects are given the vaccine, while others are given a placebo, which is a substance without any medical benefits. Saline solution is commonly used as a placebo. This will let researchers see if the vaccine actually works, has any side effects, and what dosages should be used. These trials might be non-blinded. This means that the researchers, and possibly even the subjects, know if they're getting the vaccine or a placebo.

If Phase I goes well, researchers move on to Phase II. The main difference between the first two phases is the size of the test groups. In Phase II, hundreds of subjects are given the vaccine. Some of these subjects might be from groups that are at risk of actually catching the disease. In this phase, a variety of factors are observed: the vaccine's safety, dose size, the most effective schedule, and the best method of administering it.

Volunteering for a vaccine trial can be a good way to give back to the community.

Vaccine trials take a long time because so many people are involved in making sure a product is safe. If there is a serious public health emergency, though, the FDA can fast-track a vaccine.

In Phase II trials, the distribution of the vaccine and the placebo are random.

Phase III trials are even bigger than Phase II. They often involve up to tens of thousands of people. These tests are double-blind, which means neither the subjects or the scientists administering the test know who receives the vaccine and who receives the placebo. The huge number of test subjects are also spread out over different geographic regions, to ensure that the vaccine works equally well in different kinds of people. The larger number of test subjects also allows researchers to watch for rare side effects. After all, if a vaccine only affects one in ten thousand people badly, it's unlikely to be discovered in a test group of only a few hundred individuals.

If a vaccine manages to pass the three clinical trials, the collected research is presented to the FDA. This is part of a Biologics License Application (BLA). The FDA will then review and check the data, examine the factory that manufactures the vaccine, and review the vaccine's label.

Quality controls, including FDA inspections, are part of the process of manufacturing and packaging vaccines.

PRODUCTION

Once a vaccine has been approved, it's time to begin production. Like clinical trials, production takes place over three steps. First, the antigen is generated, and then purified. Finally, the vaccine is formulated.

To generate antigens, first you have to have a pathogen to isolate them from. The method for producing these depends on the pathogen. Viruses are grown in cells like chicken eggs or in cell lines that continually reproduce. Bacteria are usually grown in bioreactors, which are devices that support the processes that allow bacteria to grow. This is also when pathogens are weakened with heat or chemicals, if it's for an attenuated vaccine.

Once the antigen has been generated, along with the pathogen, the antigen must be isolated and purified. This will get rid of most of the virus or bacteria and just leave the antigens that provoke an immune response.

When the vaccine is ready, it is put in a vial or syringe, sealed, and labeled. Then it must be shipped safely in a way that doesn't affect its effectiveness.

The last step is formulation. This is when additional ingredients are added to the vaccine. Three common additions are adjuvants, stabilizers, and preservatives. Adjuvants help create a stronger response from the immune system. Stabilizers allow the vaccine to be stored without going bad, and preservatives allow it to be used for multiple doses.

AFTER RELEASE

Even after a vaccine is released to the general public, it's still monitored and studied. These are call the Phase IV trials. These trials collect data on how well the vaccine is working in the real world, and make sure that it is not provoking any unforeseen serious adverse effects. These trials also help to refine the best time to schedule doses of the new vaccine based on outbreaks.

CHAPTER 6

VACCINES OF THE FUTURE

Every day, scientists and researchers are working to develop new vaccines that will protect humanity from a variety of dangerous diseases. Research is constantly being done on how to improve existing vaccines. Some scientists are even attempting to create vaccines against noninfectious diseases, such as cancer.

There are many diseases that scientists are hoping to develop vaccines for within the next decade. Infectious diseases that are being focused on right now include malaria, tuberculosis, and HIV/AIDS. Vaccines for these diseases will likely be similar to already existing vaccines. TB is still a very dangerous disease. It caused over a million deaths in 2011 and certain strains are becoming resistant to antibiotics. And, since some strains are incurable, the need for a vaccine that can prevent the disease is clear. The same is true of HIV/AIDS. Since there currently isn't a cure, prevention through vaccination is one of the best chances we have of stopping the spread of the disease.

UNIVERSAL FLU VACCINE

IDEALLY, ONE VACCINE WOULD PROTECT AGAINST ALL FLU STRAINS FOR MORE THAN ONE YEAR. SCIENTISTS ARE TRYING TO DEVELOP A UNIVERSAL FLU VACCINE BY TARGETING PARTS OF THE VIRUS THAT DO NOT CHANGE EACH FLU SEASON. BUT A VACCINE FOR PUBLIC USE IS YEARS AWAY.

Flu vaccine in the form of a nasal spray became popular after it was licensed by the FDA in 2003 for use in people ages 2-49. Questions arose about its effectiveness, however, and it was not recommended for the 2016-17 flu season. The FDA continues to work to determine the cause of the lower than expected effectiveness of the nasal spray flu vaccine observed in recent years.

Many people prefer a no-needle nasal flu vaccine. Either way, an inoculation is needed annually because the dominant strains of flu virus change.

There has already been some success in creating vaccines that prevent cancer. For example, the HPV vaccine protects against a virus that causes cervical cancer. While researchers are trying to find ways to vaccinate against other forms of cancer, they're also looking for ways to vaccinate against other noninfectious diseases. One example is Alzheimer's disease, which is a leading cause of dementia in the elderly. **Autoimmune** diseases such as lupus and multiple sclerosis are also being investigated. These vaccines would function differently from those created for infectious diseases. As a result, they are taking longer to create than a traditional vaccine would.

New ways of administering vaccines are also being researched. There are already some vaccines that don't require the use of a needle. Certain influenza vaccines can be inhaled, and are available in a nasal spray. Another possibility is a vaccine patch. A pattern of tiny needles on the underside of the patch would deliver the vaccine. This would eliminate the need for a syringe. This would have a few benefits: first of all, the patch wouldn't need to be administered by a trained medical professional. Places without medical facilities, or which aren't visited by doctors or nurses very often, could still give vaccinations. Secondly, it might encourage people with a fear of needles to get vaccinated when they may not have before.

Even with all the current research into alternatives, needle-based inoculation likely won't be going away for a long time.

Some day, people may simply eat their vaccines. Plants already have been genetically modified to produce antigens that trigger immune responses, but scientists are a long way from bringing such a vaccine to the public. Some early success has been found using food-based antigens against hepatitis B and a respiratory virus that affects young children. It's also expected that such vaccines will work well against diseases that cause severe diarrhea, such as cholera and norovirus.

Tomatoes, potatoes, and bananas look promising for making edible vaccines. It would be easier to store, transport, and administer food-based vaccines, so immunizing people in developing countries would become simpler and cheaper. Kids (and adults) who hate shots would be happy, too.

Plant-based vaccines also could be produced by modifying leaves to contain antigens. The leaves would be freeze-dried, ground up, and put into pill form.

The 20th century saw amazing leaps in the field of vaccination. But there are still advances to be made, and with devoted scientists continuing to do important research every day, there's no telling what the future might bring.

TIMELINE OF VACCINE DEVELOPMENT

First vaccine for smallpox (the first vaccine ever developed)
1796

First vaccine for rabies by Louis Pasteur and Émile Roux
1885

First vaccine for tetanus
1890

First vaccine for bubonic plague
1897

First vaccine for tuberculosis
1925

First vaccine for typhus
1937

First vaccine for influenza
1945

First oral polio vaccine
1961

First vaccine for adenovirus-4 and 7
1957

1954
First vaccine for human anthrax

1952
First vaccine for polio by Jonas Salk

1879
First vaccine for cholera

1896
First vaccine for typhoid fever

1932
First vaccine for yellow fever

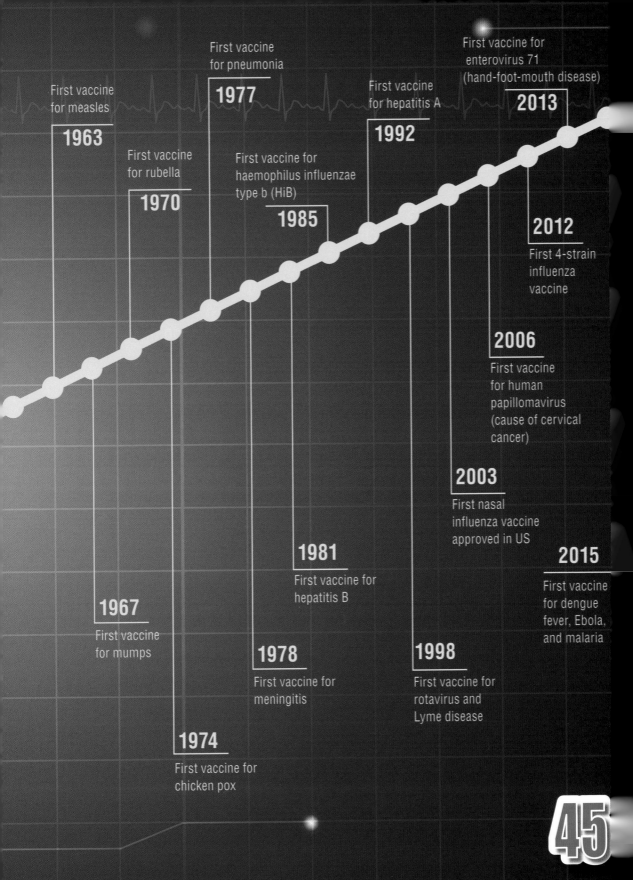

First vaccine for measles
1963

First vaccine for rubella
1970

First vaccine for pneumonia
1977

First vaccine for haemophilus influenzae type b (HiB)
1985

First vaccine for hepatitis A
1992

First vaccine for enterovirus 71 (hand-foot-mouth disease)
2013

2012
First 4-strain influenza vaccine

2006
First vaccine for human papillomavirus (cause of cervical cancer)

2003
First nasal influenza vaccine approved in US

1981
First vaccine for hepatitis B

1967
First vaccine for mumps

1978
First vaccine for meningitis

1998
First vaccine for rotavirus and Lyme disease

2015
First vaccine for dengue fever, Ebola, and malaria

1974
First vaccine for chicken pox

45

GLOSSARY

antibodies: Proteins made by the blood that attack specific disease-causing agents.

autoimmune: A type of disease that causes the immune system to attack its own body.

bacteria: Single-celled organisms that are rod, spiral, or sphere shaped, some of which can cause disease.

compromised: Weakened.

diseases: Conditions that affect living things and prevent them from functioning as well as they're normally able to.

immune system: A network of cells and processes that fights off disease in living things.

mutate: To cause genetic material to change resulting in an unusual characteristic in an organism.

organisms: All living things including plants, animals, and even single-celled life-forms.

paralysis: An inability to move all or part of the body.

patent: A type of license that enables the holder to determine who is allowed to manufacture an invention.

smallpox: A disease that presents with flu-like symptoms and red bumps on the skin.

virus: A kind of tiny parasite that can only replicate in living cells of other organisms.

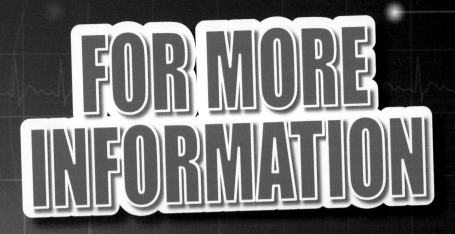

FOR MORE INFORMATION

BOOKS

Rooney, Anne. *You Wouldn't Want to Live Without Vaccinations!*
Franklin Watts, 2015.

Wood, Susan. *Vaccine Innovators Pearl Kendrick
and Grace Eldering*. Minneapolis, MN: Lerner Classroom, 2016.

Yomtov, Nel. *From African Plant to Vaccine Preservation*.
North Mankato, MN: Cherry Lake Publishing, 2014.

WEBSITES

www.cdc.gov/vaccines
Centers for Disease Control and Prevention, the national public
health institute of the United States.

www.vaccineinformation.org
Immunization Action Coalition, a national leader in
immunization education.

INDEX